Our Favorite
Retro Recipes

Copyright 2024, Gooseberry Patch

Don't forget slow cookers make great traveling companions for campers and RV'ers. Enjoy all the fun of the great outdoors, then come in for a delicious dinner.

Swiss Steak

Makes 4 to 6 servings

1-1/2 lbs. beef round steak, cut
    into serving-size pieces
2 T. all-purpose flour
1 t. salt
1/4 t. pepper

1 c. celery, chopped
1 carrot, peeled and chopped
1 onion, sliced
15-oz. can tomato sauce

Place steak in a slow cooker; set aside. Combine flour, salt and pepper; sprinkle over meat. Mix well. Add vegetables; pour tomato sauce over all. Cover and cook on low setting for 8 to 10 hours.

Keep a cherished cookbook clean and free of spatters.
Slip it into a gallon-size plastic zipping bag before cooking
up a favorite recipe.

Good Morning Monkey Bread

Makes 18 rolls

18 frozen white dinner rolls
3/4 c. sugar
3/4 c. brown sugar, packed
3-1/2 oz. pkg. cook & serve
    butterscotch pudding mix

3 to 4 t. cinnamon
1/2 c. butter, sliced
Optional: 1/2 c. chopped pecans

Scatter frozen rolls in a Bundt® pan that has been sprayed with non-stick vegetable spray. Rolls will expand, so take care not to overfill pan. Set aside. In a separate bowl, mix sugars, dry pudding mix and cinnamon together. Sprinkle mixture on top of frozen rolls; dot with butter. Cover pan with a tea towel; let rise overnight. In the morning, uncover and bake at 350 degrees for 30 to 45 minutes. Remove from oven and let stand 15 to 20 minutes. Turn pan over onto a serving tray; spoon warm syrup from pan over bread.

Post a notepad on the fridge to make a note whenever a pantry staple is used up. You'll never run out of that one item you need!

Cheddar Potato Skins

Makes 2 dozen

6 baking potatoes
1 c. finely shredded Cheddar
   cheese

2 T. green onion, finely chopped
1/8 t. garlic powder
Garnish: sour cream, salsa

Bake potatoes at 425 degrees for 40 to 50 minutes, until tender. Quarter each potato lengthwise and scoop out insides, leaving 1/2-inch thick shells. Arrange potato shells skin-side up on an ungreased baking sheet; spray skins evenly with non-stick vegetable spray. Bake, uncovered, at 425 degrees for 20 to 25 minutes, until crisp. Turn shells skin-side down. Toss together cheese, onion and garlic powder; sprinkle evenly over shells. Return to oven for an additional 2 minutes, until cheese melts. Serve with sour cream and salsa.

Serving soup as a first course before the main dish?
Allow one cup per guest. When serving hearty soup
as the main dish, allow 2 cups per guest.

French Onion Soup

1 t. butter
2 t. olive oil
4 onions, sliced
3 c. beef broth

3 to 4 bay leaves
salt and pepper to taste
6 slices French bread
3/4 c. shredded Swiss cheese

Heat butter and oil together in a stockpot until butter melts. Add onions; cook over medium heat for 20 to 30 minutes, until dark golden. Add broth, bay leaves, salt and pepper. Bring to a boil; reduce heat, cover and simmer for 30 minutes. Remove and discard bay leaves; set aside. Arrange bread on an ungreased broiler pan; sprinkle with cheese and broil until golden. Divide soup among 6 soup bowls; top each with a slice of toasted bread.

Patio chats can last well into the evening, so set out
twinkling votives nestled inside colorful retro drinking
glasses. Add some sea salt crystals inside the
glasses...they'll steady the votives and add sparkle.

Swedish Meatballs

Makes 2 to 3 dozen

2 lbs. ground beef
1 c. cracker crumbs
2 eggs, beaten
1 t. garlic, minced
1/2 t. salt
1 T. olive oil

10-3/4 oz. can cream of
    mushroom soup
10-3/4 oz. can cream of
    chicken soup
1/2 c. plus 2 T. milk

Combine ground beef, crumbs, eggs, garlic and salt; mix well and shape into one-inch balls. Brown meatballs in olive oil in a skillet; drain. Arrange meatballs in an ungreased 13"x9" baking pan; set aside. Combine soups and milk; blend well and pour over meatballs. Cover and bake at 350 degrees until bubbly, about 25 minutes.

A tin lunchbox is perfect for storing favorite recipes.

Down-Home Tuna Casserole

Makes 4 servings

8-oz. pkg. medium egg
    noodles, cooked
2 T. butter
1 c. celery, chopped
1/4 c. onion, chopped
10-3/4 oz. can cream of
    mushroom soup
3/4 c. milk

2 T. all-purpose flour
1/4 t. dried thyme
1/4 t. pepper
9-1/4 oz. can tuna, drained
1 sleeve round buttery crackers,
    crushed
1/4 c. grated Parmesan cheese

Place cooked noodles in a greased 1-1/2 quart casserole dish; set aside. Melt butter in a small saucepan over medium heat. Sauté celery and onion until tender; stir into noodles. Blend soup, milk, flour and seasonings in a small bowl; add tuna. Combine with noodles; mix well. Toss together crushed crackers and Parmesan cheese; sprinkle over top. Bake at 350 degrees for 25 minutes.

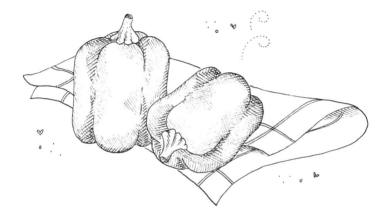

Slice & dice meats and veggies ahead of time and refrigerate in separate plastic zipping bags. In the morning, toss everything into the slow cooker and you're on your way.

Homestyle Stuffed Peppers

Makes 4 servings

1-1/2 lbs. ground beef
1 onion, finely chopped
1 c. long-cooking rice,
    uncooked

4 green peppers, tops removed
15-oz. can tomato sauce
Optional: salt-free herb
    seasoning to taste

Mix together ground beef, onion and rice; spoon into peppers. Arrange peppers in a slow cooker; pour tomato sauce over top. Sprinkle with seasoning, if desired. Cover and cook on low setting for 5 to 6 hours.

Shake up a simple vinaigrette dressing. Combine 2 tablespoons cider vinegar, 6 tablespoons olive oil and one teaspoon Dijon mustard in a small jar, twist on the lid and shake well. Add salt and pepper to taste.

Grandma's Waldorf Salad

Serves 6

2 Gala apples, cored and diced
1 Granny Smith apple, cored
   and diced
1/2 c. chopped pecans or walnuts

1/2 c. celery, diced
1/3 c. sweetened dried cranberries
1/3 c. mayonnaise

Stir together all ingredients in a large bowl. Cover and chill until serving time.

Place packets of flower seeds in a basket by your front
door...let guests pick their favorites to take home.
As the flowers bloom, friends will be reminded of you.

Garlic Deviled Eggs

Makes 12 servings

6 eggs, hard-boiled and peeled
1/3 c. mayonnaise
1/2 to 1 t. mustard
1 t. pickle relish

1 onion, chopped
1 clove garlic, minced
1/8 t. salt
Garnish: paprika

Slice eggs in half lengthwise; remove yolks, setting aside egg whites. In a mixing bowl, mash yolks with a fork. Add remaining ingredients except paprika; mix well. Spoon yolk mixture into egg whites; sprinkle with paprika. Chill.

Cook a double batch of rice, then freeze half in a plastic
freezer bag for another meal. When you're ready to use
the frozen rice, just microwave on high for one minute per
cup to thaw, 2 to 3 minutes per cup to warm it through.
Fluff with a fork...ready to use!

Jammin' Jambalaya

Serves 10 to 12

1 lb. boneless, skinless chicken
    breasts, cubed
1 lb. andouille sausage, sliced
28-oz. can diced tomatoes
1 onion, chopped
1 green pepper, chopped
1 c. celery, chopped
1 c. chicken broth

2 t. Cajun seasoning
2 t. dried oregano
2 t. dried parsley
1 t. cayenne pepper
1/2 t. dried thyme
1 lb. frozen cooked shrimp,
    thawed and tails removed
cooked rice

Place chicken, sausage, tomatoes, onion, pepper, celery and broth in a slow cooker. Stir in seasonings; mix well. Cover and cook for 7 to 8 hours on low setting, or 3 to 4 hours on high setting. Add shrimp during final 30 minutes of cooking time. Serve over cooked rice.

For a pretty brunch table setting, lay a red and white quilt on
your breakfast table. Fill a watering can with wildflowers
and tie a cheery red gingham bow to the handle.
Serve breakfast on old-fashioned spatterware plates.

Cinnamon Streusel Coffee Cake   *Makes 15 servings*

3-1/4 c. all-purpose flour,
    divided
2 T. baking powder
1/2 t. salt
1-1/2 c. sugar
3/4 c. butter, divided

2 eggs, beaten
1 c. milk
2 t. vanilla extract
1 c. brown sugar, packed
4 t. cinnamon

Mix 3 cups flour, baking powder, salt and sugar in a large bowl. Cut in 1/2 cup butter until mixture resembles cornmeal. Blend in eggs, milk and vanilla; stir just enough to combine thoroughly. Spread evenly into a greased and floured 13"x9" baking pan. For topping, mix brown sugar, remaining flour and cinnamon; melt remaining butter and stir in. Sprinkle topping over batter; bake at 375 degrees for 25 to 30 minutes. Cut into squares; serve warm.

Eggs work best in baking recipes when they're brought to room temperature first. If time is short, just slip the eggs carefully into a bowl of lukewarm water and let stand for 15 minutes...they'll warm right up.

Peanut Butter Kiss Cookies

Makes 12 to 15 cookies

1 c. creamy peanut butter
1 egg, beaten
1 c. sugar

12 to 15 milk chocolate drops
unwrapped

In a bowl, mix together peanut butter, egg and sugar; roll into 1-inch balls. Place on an ungreased baking sheet. Bake at 250 degrees for 6 to 7 minutes. Remove from oven; top each cookie with a chocolate drop. Cool completely.

Slow cookers are ideal for any country supper potluck.
Tote them filled with your favorite spiced cider, shredded
chicken, hearty stew or cobbler...scrumptious!

Chicken & Dumplin' Soup

Serves 6 to 8

10-3/4 oz. can cream of chicken soup
4 c. chicken broth
4 boneless, skinless chicken breasts, cooked and shredded

2 15-oz. cans mixed vegetables
12-oz. tube refrigerated biscuits, quartered
Optional: pepper to taste

Combine soup and broth in a 6-quart stockpot; bring to a boil over medium-high heat, whisking until smooth. Stir in chicken and vegetables; bring to a boil. Drop biscuit quarters into soup; cover and simmer for 15 minutes. Let soup stand for 10 minutes before serving. Sprinkle each serving with pepper, if desired.

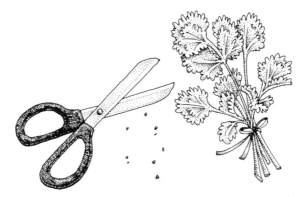

Kitchen shears are oh-so handy for snipping fresh herbs,
chopping green onions and snipping the ends off fresh
green beans. Just remember to wash them with
soap and water after each use.

Spinach, Strawberry & Walnut Salad

Makes 6 servings

1-1/2 lbs. spinach, torn
3 c. strawberries, hulled and
    sliced

1 sweet onion, thinly sliced
1 c. chopped walnuts

Arrange spinach, strawberries, onions and nuts in a salad bowl. Cover and refrigerate. At serving time, drizzle desired amount of Poppy Seed Dressing over salad. Toss and serve immediately.

Poppy Seed Dressing:

3/4 c. sugar
1 t. dry mustard
1 t. salt
1/3 c. cider vinegar

2 t. green onion, chopped
3/4 to 1 c. olive oil
1-1/2 T. poppy seed

In a blender, mix sugar, mustard, salt and vinegar until smooth. Add onion and blend until smooth. With blender running, add oil slowly. Blend until thick. Stir in poppy seed.

Spoon leftover Speedy Spanish Rice into
flour tortillas for a yummy quick lunch.

Speedy Spanish Rice

Serves 6

1 c. long-cooking rice, uncooked
1/2 c. onion, chopped
2 T. oil
2 c. chicken broth
3/4 c. tomato juice

1/2 t. garlic powder
1/2 t. chili powder
1/2 t. ground cumin
1/3 c. fresh cilantro, chopped

In a skillet over medium heat, sauté rice and onion in oil until onion is crisp-tender, about 5 minutes. Add remaining ingredients except cilantro. Bring to a boil; reduce heat and cover. Simmer for 15 to 20 minutes, or until liquid is absorbed. Fluff rice with a fork; fold in cilantro.

Cubed, cooked chicken can be purchased in vacuum-sealed foil pouches...just open and use in your favorite recipe.

Chicken Cordon Bleu

Serves 4 to 6

4 to 6 boneless, skinless
   chicken breasts
4 to 6 thin slices deli ham
4 to 6 slices Swiss cheese

10-3/4 oz. can cream of
   mushroom soup
1/4 c. milk

Place each chicken breast in a plastic zipping bag. Flatten to 1/4-inch thick; remove from bag. Top each with a slice of ham and a slice of cheese; roll up and secure with a toothpick. Arrange rolls in a slow cooker in layers. Mix together soup and milk; pour over chicken. Cover and cook on low setting for 4 to 6 hours, until chicken is no longer pink inside. To serve, remove toothpicks and arrange chicken rolls on serving plate; spoon sauce from slow cooker over rolls.

For an extra-special treat, pour melted chocolate onto wax paper-lined cookie sheets and spread to 1/8-inch thickness. Refrigerate until firm and then cut shapes with mini cookie cutters. Remove from wax paper and chill. Garnish cakes, pies, even Chocolate Chip Waffles!

Chocolate Chip Waffles

Makes 6 servings

1-3/4 c. all-purpose flour
2 t. baking powder
1/2 t. salt
1-1/2 c. milk
1 T. butter, melted

1-1/2 t. vanilla extract
1 egg, separated
1 T. sugar
1/2 c. mini semi-sweet
   chocolate chips

Combine the flour, baking powder and salt in a large bowl; set aside. Whisk together milk, butter, vanilla and egg yolk until frothy; add to flour mixture, stirring well. Set aside. Beat egg white and sugar until stiff peaks form; fold into flour mixture. Gently stir in chocolate chips. Pour by 1/2 cupfuls onto a hot, greased waffle iron; cook according to manufacturer's instructions.

Try red pepper strips, endive leaves, cucumber slices and snow peas as fresh and tasty alternatives to potato chips for scooping up creamy dips!

So-Good Spinach Dip

Makes about 3 cups

12-oz. container low-fat cottage
    cheese
1 c. reduced-fat mayonnaise
1 T. lemon juice
1.4-oz. env. vegetable soup mix
1 T. onion, grated

10-oz. pkg. frozen spinach,
    thawed and drained
8-oz. can water chestnuts,
    drained and chopped
reduced-fat snack crackers or
    sliced vegetables

Spoon cottage cheese into a blender; blend until smooth. Spoon into a bowl; combine with mayonnaise, lemon juice, soup mix, onion, spinach and water chestnuts. Mix well and chill. Serve with crackers or vegetables for dipping.

Invite family & friends to a Sunday afternoon dessert social!
Everyone brings a pie, a cake or another favorite dessert...
you provide the ice cream and whipped topping.

Apple Cream Crumb Cake

Makes 9 servings

18-1/2 oz. pkg. yellow cake mix
1/4 c. butter, softened
2 eggs, divided
1 c. sour cream

21-oz. can apple pie filling
1/3 c. brown sugar, packed
1 t. cinnamon

In a large bowl, combine cake mix, butter and one egg; mix until crumbly. Reserve 1/2 cup of mixture for topping. Press remaining crumb mixture into a greased 8"x8" baking pan. In a small bowl, blend remaining egg with sour cream; spoon over crust. In another bowl, combine pie filling, brown sugar and cinnamon; spoon over sour cream mixture. Top with reserved crumb mixture. Bake at 350 degrees for 40 minutes, or until filling is bubbly and topping is lightly golden. Cool; cut into squares.

Set up a topping bar when making pizza...everyone can just help themselves by adding their favorite toppings to individual servings.

French Bread Sausage Pizza

Makes 6 to 8 servings

1 loaf French bread, halved
   lengthwise
15-oz. can pizza sauce
1 lb. ground pork sausage,
   browned and drained

3-1/2 oz. pkg. sliced pepperoni
8-oz. pkg. shredded mozzarella
   cheese

Place both halves of loaf on an ungreased baking sheet, cut-side up.
Spread with pizza sauce; top with sausage, pepperoni and cheese. Bake
at 350 degrees for 15 minutes, or until cheese is melted. Slice to serve.

Get together with a girlfriend or two and spend a day making double batches of favorite casseroles to freeze. Your freezers will be full in no time!

Ham & Cheese Pinwheels

Makes 16 servings

16-oz. pkg. hot roll mix
1/4 c. butter, softened
1-oz. pkg. ranch salad
    dressing mix

1 c. shredded Cheddar cheese
1/2 lb. thinly sliced deli ham

Prepare hot roll mix according to package directions; knead dough 10 times on a well-floured surface. Roll into an 18-inch by 12-inch rectangle; set aside. Mix butter and dressing mix; spread on dough. Sprinkle with cheese; arrange ham slices over cheese. Starting at long edge of dough, roll up jelly-roll style. Pinch raw edges together; place seam-side down on a greased baking sheet. Pinch ends together. Snip top of dough at 2-inch intervals. Cover and let rise until double in bulk, 45 minutes to one hour. Bake at 325 degrees for 40 to 50 minutes, until golden. Slice to serve.

Add a few extra cloves of garlic to the pan when cooking pasta.
Combine the extra garlic with 1/2 cup softened butter.
Mix well and chill. Spread on thick slices of Italian bread
and broil for a few minutes until crunchy and golden.

Easy Goulash

Makes 4 to 6 servings

1 lb. ground beef
1/4 c. onion, chopped
14-1/2 oz. can stewed tomatoes
3/4 c. water
2 c. elbow macaroni, uncooked
salt and pepper to taste

15-1/4 oz. can corn, drained
15-oz. can kidney beans,
  drained and rinsed
16-oz. pkg. pasteurized process
  cheese spread, cubed

Brown beef and onion in a large saucepan over medium heat; drain and return to pan. Stir in tomatoes, water, uncooked macaroni, salt and pepper to taste. Simmer, stirring occasionally, for 8 to 10 minutes, until macaroni is tender. Add corn, beans and cheese; continue cooking until heated through and cheese is melted.

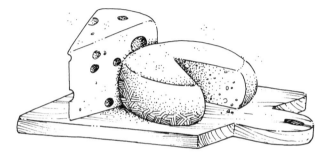

Serve a variety of different cheeses at your brunch...perfect
for guests to nibble on! Line a white-washed basket with red
and white homespun, tie a red ticking bow on the handle and fill
it with an assortment of cheeses and crackers.

Cranberry Scones

Makes 16 scones

2-1/2 c. all-purpose flour
2-1/2 t. baking powder
1/2 t. baking soda
3/4 c. butter, sliced
1 c. cranberries, chopped

2/3 c. sugar
3/4 c. buttermilk
2/3 c. powdered sugar
1 T. warm water
1/4 t. vanilla extract

Mix flour, baking powder and baking soda together in a large bowl; cut in butter until mixture resembles coarse crumbs. Stir in cranberries and sugar; add buttermilk, mixing until just blended. Divide dough in half; on a floured surface, roll each portion into an 8-inch circle, about 1/2-inch thick. Cut each circle into 8 wedges; arrange on ungreased baking sheets. Bake at 400 degrees for 12 to 15 minutes; remove to a wire rack. Combine powdered sugar, warm water and vanilla in a small bowl. Mix to a drizzling consistency, adding a little more warm water if necessary. Drizzle glaze over scones; serve warm.

The best thing about the farmers' market...everything is locally grown, in season. Plump strawberries are ready in June blueberries and beans in July; corn, melons and peaches in August; and apples and pumpkins in October. Enjoy!

Over-Stuffed Mushrooms

Serves 4 to 6

1 lb. mushrooms
3 T. grated Parmesan cheese
1 clove garlic, pressed
1 onion, finely chopped
1 c. dry bread crumbs

1 T. fresh parsley, minced
2 T. butter, melted
salt and pepper to taste
6 T. oil, divided

Remove stems from mushrooms; set aside. In a bowl, mix remaining ingredients except oil; spoon into mushroom caps. Spread 2 tablespoons oil in a 13"x9" baking pan; arrange mushrooms in pan. Drizzle remaining oil evenly over mushrooms; bake at 350 degrees for 20 minutes. Serve warm.

Dress up the dinner table with some vintage whimsies!
While on vacation, check out local flea markets for
salt & pepper shakers in unusual shapes...dancing fruit,
hula girls and animals of all shapes and sizes will
really spark dinnertime conversations!

Country-Style Reuben

Makes one sandwich

2 slices rye bread
2 t. butter, softened
1 slice Swiss cheese
2 to 3 slices deli corned beef

2 to 3 T. sauerkraut, drained
1 to 2 T. Thousand Island salad
   dressing

Butter one side of each bread slice. Place bread butter-side down into each side of pie iron. Layer remaining ingredients on one bread slice; carefully close pie iron. Grill over coals for 3 to 5 minutes on each side.

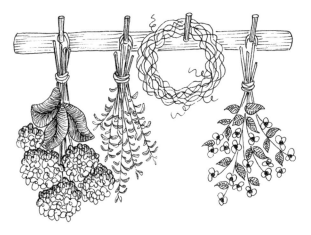

Add freshly snipped herbs like basil, dill or thyme
to biscuit dough for delicious variety.

Onion Dinner Rolls

Makes 6 servings

1/2 c. butter, melted
1-1/2 t. dried parsley
1/2 t. dill weed
1 T. dried, minced onion

2 T. grated Parmesan cheese
10-oz. tube refrigerated
    buttermilk biscuits

Place melted butter in a bowl; stir in herbs, onion and Parmesan cheese. Cut each biscuit into quarters; dip into butter mixture, coating all sides. Arrange biscuits in a greased 9"x9" baking pan; bake at 425 degrees for 15 minutes.

Before you head out with the family, cut cookie bars, brownies, crispy rice treats or fudge into individual servings at home. Place ooey-gooey treats in mini plastic zipping bags to share later...no more sticky fingers!

Jo Ann's Chocolate-Caramel Pudding

Serves 6

2 3.9-oz. pkgs. instant chocolate pudding mix
4 c. milk

12 lady fingers
garnish: caramel ice cream
  topping

Mix together pudding mixes and milk for 3 minutes; spoon into individual plastic cups. Top each with 2 ladyfingers; drizzle with caramel topping. Serve immediately or chill.

Fill up a big party tray with fresh veggies as a handy side dish for sandwiches. Any extras can be tossed into a crunchy salad the next day.

Uncle Joe's Sloppy Joes

Serves 6 to 8

2 lbs. ground beef
1 onion, chopped
1/2 c. green pepper, chopped
1/2 c. celery, chopped
2 14-1/2 oz. cans stewed
   tomatoes
2 c. tomato sauce

1/2 c. catsup
1/4 c. brown sugar, packed
2 T. spicy mustard
1 T. Worcestershire sauce
1/4 t. salt
1/4 t. pepper
6 to 8 sandwich buns, split

Brown ground beef, onion, green pepper and celery in a large skillet over medium heat; drain. Add remaining ingredients except buns. Bring to a boil; reduce heat and simmer for one hour, stirring occasionally. Spoon onto buns and serve.

Vintage magazine recipe ads make fun wall art for
the kitchen. They're easy to find at flea markets...look for
ones featuring shimmery gelatin salads, golden mac & cheese
or other favorites like Mom used to make!

Dad's Best Mac & Cheese

Makes 6 to 8 servings

8-oz. pkg. elbow macaroni,
    uncooked
1 egg, beaten
1 T. hot water
1 t. dry mustard

1 t. salt
1 c. milk
12-oz. pkg. shredded sharp
    Cheddar cheese, divided
1 T. butter, softened

Cook macaroni according to package directions; drain and return to pan. Whisk egg, water, mustard and salt together; add to macaroni. Pour in milk and stir well. Add most of cheese, reserving enough to sprinkle on top. Spread butter in a 2-quart casserole dish; pour macaroni mixture into dish. Sprinkle with reserved cheese. Bake, uncovered, at 350 degrees for 35 to 45 minutes, until top is golden.

Soup suppers are a fuss-free way to get together with friends, neighbors and family. Each family brings a favorite soup to share, along with the recipe. What a delicious way to try a variety of soups!

Grandma's Creamy Potato Soup

Makes 4 servings

5 potatoes, peeled and cut into
    bite-size cubes
12-oz. can evaporated milk
1-1/2 c. whole milk
1-1/2 c. water
1/2 c. butter, sliced

1 onion, quartered
1 stalk celery, chopped
garlic juice or powder to taste
1 t. salt
1/2 t. pepper

Place potatoes in a stockpot; add milks and water. Bring to a simmer over medium heat. Add butter; allow to melt. Add remaining ingredients; stir until well blended. Reduce heat to low; do not allow soup to boil. Simmer until potatoes are soft.

Tuck odds & ends of leftover sliced bread, croissants
and even cinnamon rolls into a freezer container. Before long,
you'll have enough for delicious French toast!

Golden French Toast

Serves 8 to 10

1 loaf white bread, cubed
   and divided
8-oz. pkg. cream cheese, softened and cubed

10 eggs, beaten
1-1/2 c. half-and-half
1/2 c. butter, melted
1/4 c. maple syrup

Layer half the bread in a greased 13"x9" baking pan; top with cream cheese. Place remaining bread over the top; set aside. Beat eggs, half-and-half, butter and syrup together; pour over bread. Refrigerate overnight; bake at 350 degrees for 40 to 50 minutes.

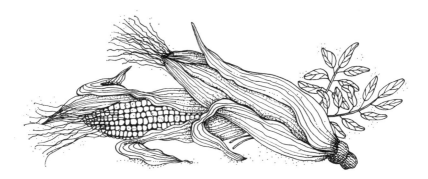

Toting a casserole to a get-together? Wrap it up in
a cheery bandanna and tie the knot at the top...an ideal spot
to slip in a serving spoon!

Cornbread Corn Casserole   *Makes 15 to 18 servings*

8-1/2 oz. pkg. corn muffin mix
2 15-oz. cans creamed corn
1 egg, beaten

1/3 c. butter, melted
3/4 c. sour cream

Combine ingredients; pour into a greased 13"x9" baking pan. Bake at
375 degrees for 35 to 45 minutes.

Mix up some salsa in a jiffy! Pour a 15-ounce can of stewed tomatoes, several slices of canned jalapeños and a teaspoon or 2 of the jalapeño juice into a blender. Cover and process to the desired consistency.

Hot & Melty Taco Dip

Makes 8 servings

16-oz. can refried beans
1-1/2 oz. pkg. taco seasoning
   mix
16-oz. container sour cream
8-oz. pkg. cream cheese,
   softened
16-oz. jar salsa

8-oz. pkg. shredded sharp
   Cheddar cheese
Garnish: shredded lettuce,
   chopped tomatoes, sliced
   black olives, jalapeño peppers,
   green onions
scoop-type tortilla chips

In a bowl, combine refried beans with taco seasoning. Spread in the bottom of a lightly greased 13"x9" glass baking pan; set aside. In a separate bowl, blend sour cream and cream cheese; spread over bean layer. Spoon salsa over sour cream layer; sprinkle cheese on top. Bake, uncovered, at 350 degrees for about 25 minutes, until beans are warmed through and cheese is melted. Garnish with desired toppings. Serve warm with tortilla chips.

There is nothing better on a cold wintry day than a
properly made pot pie.
-Craig Claiborne

Chicken Pot Pie

Serves 4 to 6

2 c. cooked chicken, chopped
15-oz. can mixed vegetables,
   drained
2 10-3/4 oz. cans cream of
   chicken soup

1 c. milk
10-oz. tube refrigerated
   biscuits, quartered

Combine first 4 ingredients together; place in an ungreased 3-quart casserole dish. Bake at 400 degrees for 20 minutes. Arrange biscuit pieces on top of hot chicken mixture; bake, uncovered, until golden, about 15 minutes.

Dress up a dessert tray in no time for a grand ending to your party! Place Mocha Truffles in bright red or gold foil candy cups.

Mocha Truffles

Makes 5 to 6 dozen

2 12-oz. pkgs. semi-sweet
  chocolate chips
8-oz. pkg. cream cheese,
  softened

3 T. instant coffee granules
2 t. water
16-oz. pkg. dark chocolate
  melting chocolate, chopped

Place chocolate chips in a microwave-safe bowl. Microwave on high setting at 30-second intervals until melted; stir until smooth. Add cream cheese, coffee granules and water; mix well with an electric mixer on medium setting. Chill until firm enough to shape; form into one-inch balls and place on wax paper-lined baking sheets. Chill for an additional one to 2 hours, until firm. Place melting chocolate in a microwave-safe bowl; melt as for chocolate chips. Use a small fork or dipping tool to dip balls in melted chocolate. Return to wax paper-lined baking sheets to set.

Serve individual-size omelets...pour your ingredients into lightly greased muffin cups and bake as usual.

Sunny Morn Baked Omelet

Makes 6 to 8 servings

12 thick slices country-style
   bread
6 slices deli ham
6 slices American cheese
8 eggs

3 c. milk
1 t. dry mustard
1 t. salt
1/2 c. butter, melted
1 c. corn flake cereal, crushed

Arrange 6 slices bread in the bottom of a greased 13"x9" baking pan; arrange ham and cheese slices on top. Arrange remaining bread slices over cheese; set aside. Combine eggs, milk, mustard and salt; beat well and pour over bread. Cover and refrigerate overnight. Mix together butter and cereal; sprinkle over top. Bake at 350 degrees for 45 minutes.

Freeze homemade mashed potatoes in individual muffin cups.
Once they're frozen, pop them out, store in plastic
freezer bags and microwave as needed.

Spicy Fried Chicken

Serves 6 to 8

2 c. all-purpose flour
2 T. Cajun seasoning
1-1/2 t. garlic powder
1-1/2 t. onion powder
1 T. salt

1-1/2 t. pepper
4 eggs, beaten
1/4 to 1/2 c. milk
6 lbs. chicken
oil for frying

Combine flour and seasonings in a large plastic zipping bag; set aside.
Whisk together eggs and milk. Shake chicken in flour mixture, then
dip in egg mixture. Heat 1/4 inch oil in a large skillet over medium
heat. Fry chicken until golden. Reduce heat and cook until juices run
clear, turning several times, about 30 minutes.

There's nothing cozier than tomato soup and grilled cheese
for supper! Just for fun, make grilled cheese
sandwiches in a waffle iron.

Homestyle Tomato-Basil Soup   *Makes 10 servings*

1/2 c. butter
1 c. fresh basil, chopped
2   28-oz. cans crushed
    tomatoes

2 cloves garlic, minced
4 c. half-and-half
Garnish: croutons, grated
    Parmesan cheese

Melt butter over medium heat in a large saucepan. Add basil; sauté for 2 minutes. Add tomatoes and garlic; simmer for an additional 20 minutes. Remove from heat; let stand until just warm. Transfer mixture to a blender and purée in batches. Strain into a clean pan; add half-and-half, mixing very well. Reheat soup over medium-low heat. Garnish with croutons and sprinkle with Parmesan cheese.

Fresh-baked bread and biscuits are just asking for a pat of
herb butter. Blend 1/2 cup softened butter and a teaspoon each
of chopped fresh parsley, chives and dill. Spoon into a crock
and keep chilled.

Corn Fritters

Makes one dozen

2 c. fresh or frozen corn,
   cooked
1 egg, beaten
1 T. baking powder

2 c. all-purpose flour
1 T. sugar
1 t. salt
shortening for frying

In a bowl, combine corn, egg and baking powder. In a separate bowl, mix remaining ingredients except shortening. Add flour mixture to corn mixture; stir until moistened. Melt shortening 1/2-inch deep in a skillet over medium-high heat. With a small cookie scoop, add batter to skillet, a few at a time. Cook about 5 minutes on each side, until golden. Drain on a paper towel-lined plate until ready to serve.

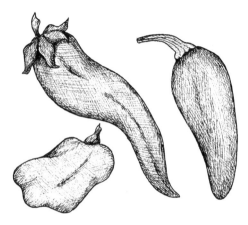

Give extra taste to recipes that use cream cheese by trying one that's flavored...chive, garlic, jalapeño or sun-dried tomato. Yummy!

Hot Crab Dip

Makes about 4 cups

3 8-oz. pkgs. cream cheese,
    cubed and softened
1/4 to 1/2 c. milk
2 6-1/2 oz. cans crabmeat,
    drained

1/2 c. green onion, chopped
1 t. prepared horseradish
1-1/2 t. Worcestershire sauce
assorted snack crackers

Combine all ingredients except crackers in a lightly greased slow cooker. Cover and cook on high setting for about 30 minutes, or until cheese melts; stir occasionally. Continue to cook on high until mixture is smooth and cheese is melted. Add more milk if necessary; turn to low setting and cook for 3 to 4 hours. Serve with crackers for dipping.

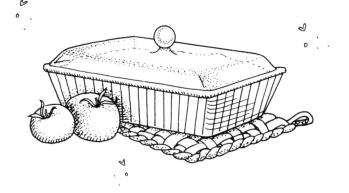

Did you know you can freeze casseroles baked or unbaked?
Let the surface freeze first, then wrap the entire pan with
plastic wrap or aluminum foil. Don't forget to add
extra cooking time to the directions.

Johnny Marzetti

1 lb. ground beef
1 onion, chopped
4-oz. can sliced mushrooms,
   drained
1/8 t. garlic salt
pepper to taste
1-1/2 T. sugar

2 15-oz. cans tomato sauce
1 T. Worcestershire sauce
8-oz. pkg. wide egg noodles,
   cooked and divided
8-oz. pkg. shredded sharp
   Cheddar cheese, divided

Cook ground beef, onion and mushrooms in a large skillet over medium heat; drain. Stir in garlic salt, pepper, sugar and sauces; simmer over low heat for 30 minutes. Layer half the noodles in a greased 2-quart casserole dish. Follow with a layer each of sauce and shredded cheese. Repeat layers. Bake, uncovered, at 375 degrees for 20 to 30 minutes.

Try something new...warm apple pie filling is delicious
spooned over individual bowls of oatmeal.

Amish Baked Oatmeal

Serves 6 to 8

1/4 c. butter, softened
1 egg, beaten
1/2 c. sugar
1 t. baking powder
1/2 t. salt

1/2 c. milk
1 t. vanilla extract
2 T. oil
1-3/4 c. quick-cooking oats,
  uncooked

Mix together all ingredients except oats until smooth; pour into a greased
13"x9" baking pan. Stir in oats. Bake, uncovered, at 350 degrees for
30 to 35 minutes.

An open home, an open heart,
here grows a bountiful harvest.

−Judy Hand

Butterball Biscuits

Makes one dozen

1/2 c. butter, melted and divided 1 t. salt
2 c. all-purpose flour 1/3 c. butter, softened
1 T. baking powder 3/4 c. milk

Spoon one teaspoon melted butter into each of 12 muffin cups; set aside
remaining melted butter. In a large bowl, sift together flour, baking
powder and salt. Add softened butter; cut in with a pastry blender until
mixture resembles cornmeal. Stir in milk with a fork. Fill each muffin
cup nearly to the top with batter. Bake at 450 degrees for 10 minutes.
Spoon one teaspoon remaining melted butter over each biscuit; bake for
10 minutes more.

Dip to go! Spoon some creamy vegetable dip into a tall plastic cup and add crunchy celery and carrot sticks, red pepper strips, cucumber slices and snow pea pods. Add a lid and the snack is ready to tote. Be sure to keep it chilled.

Homemade Guacamole

6 ripe avocados, pitted and peeled
2 to 4 cloves garlic, minced
1 lime, halved and divided
1 tomato, diced
1/2 onion, diced

salt to taste
Optional: 1 diced jalapeño pepper,
   chopped fresh cilantro
tortilla chips

Combine avocados, garlic and juice of 1/2 lime in a large bowl; mash to desired consistency. Gently stir in tomato, onion, salt and juice of remaining 1/2 lime; add jalapeño and cilantro, if using. Cover and chill for 30 minutes to one hour; stir before serving. Serve with tortilla chips.

Slow-cooker gravy...it's oh-so easy! When the meat is removed from the cooker, leave any juices inside. Make a smooth paste of 1/4 cup flour or cornstarch and 1/4 cup water. Pour into the slow cooker and stir well. Turn the cooker to the high setting and cook for 15 minutes once the mixture comes to a boil.

Diner-Style Burgers

Makes 8 servings

2 lbs. ground beef
1 egg, beaten
1 c. onion, finely chopped
1/2 c. shredded Cheddar cheese
2 T. catsup
2 T. evaporated milk

1/2 c. cracker crumbs
salt and pepper to taste
1 c. all-purpose flour
2 to 3 T. oil
10-3/4 oz. can cream of
    mushroom soup

Mix together ground beef, egg, onion, cheese, catsup, milk, cracker crumbs, salt and pepper. Shape into 8 patties; roll in flour. Heat oil in a large skillet over medium heat; brown patties. Arrange patties in a slow cooker alternately with soup. Cover and cook on high setting for 3 to 4 hours.

A cherished family recipe can be a super conversation starter. Take time to share family stories and traditions with your kids over the dinner table!

Granny's Sweet Potato Casserole

Serves 6

2-1/2 lbs. sweet potatoes, peeled
   and cubed
3/4 c. brown sugar, packed
1/4 c. butter, softened
1-1/2 t. salt

1/2 t. vanilla extract
1/2 c. pecans, finely chopped
   and divided
2 c. mini marshmallows

In a Dutch oven, cover sweet potatoes with cold water. Bring to a
boil over high heat; reduce heat to medium. Simmer for 15 minutes,
or until very tender; drain. Transfer potatoes to a large bowl and cool
slightly. Add brown sugar, butter, salt and vanilla; mash mixture
with a potato masher. Fold in 1/4 cup pecans. Spread evenly in an
11"x7" baking pan coated with non-stick vegetable spray. Sprinkle
with remaining pecans; top with marshmallows. Bake, uncovered,
at 375 degrees for 25 minutes, or until golden.

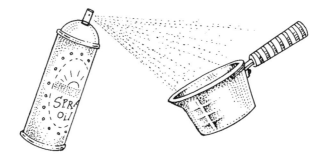

When measuring sticky ingredients like honey or peanut butter, spray the measuring cup with non-stick vegetable spray first. The contents will slip right out and you'll get a more accurate measurement.

Favorite Cocoa No-Bakes

Makes 2-1/2 to 3 dozen

3 c. quick-cooking oats, uncooked
2 c. sugar
1/2 c. butter, softened

1/2 c. milk
1/3 c. baking cocoa
2/3 c. creamy peanut butter
2 t. vanilla extract

Add oats to a blender and pulse until fine; set aside. Combine sugar, butter, milk and cocoa in a saucepan over medium heat. Bring to a rolling boil, stirring constantly. Remove from heat. Add peanut butter and vanilla; stir until smooth. Add oats and stir well. Let stand for 10 minutes. Drop mixture by rounded tablespoonfuls onto aluminum foil-lined baking sheets; cool until set.

Look for festive sombreros at party supply stores...line with brightly colored cloth napkins and serve up tortilla chips in style!

Tex-Mex Chili

Makes 4 servings

1 lb. ground beef, browned
   and drained
15-oz. can hot chili beans
15-1/2 oz. can kidney beans

12-oz. jar salsa
1-1/4 oz. pkg. chili seasoning
   mix
1/2 to 1 c. water

Combine all ingredients in a large stockpot. Bring to a boil over
medium heat; reduce heat and simmer for 10 to 15 minutes.

Make a party tray of savory bite-size appetizer tarts...
guests will never suspect how easy it is! Bake frozen mini
phyllo shells according to package directions. Cool,
then spoon in a favorite creamy dip or spread.

Bacon-Wrapped Water Chestnuts

Serves 12

2 8-oz. cans water chestnuts,
   drained
1 lb. bacon, each slice cut into
   3 pieces

1/2 c. brown sugar, packed
1/2 c. catsup

Wrap each water chestnut in a piece of bacon; fasten with a wooden toothpick. Arrange on a baking sheet coated with non-stick vegetable spray. Bake at 400 degrees for 45 minutes to one hour, until bacon is crisp. Combine brown sugar and catsup in a bowl; spoon over chestnuts. Reduce oven to 350 degrees; bake for an additional 30 to 45 minutes, until glazed.

Toast buns slightly before adding shredded or sliced meat,
for sausages or sandwiches...it only takes a minute
and makes such a tasty difference.

County Fair Italian Sausages

Makes 5 sandwiches

19.76-oz. pkg. Italian pork
   sausages
1 green pepper, sliced
1 onion, sliced

26-oz. jar pasta sauce
5 sub buns, split
Garnish: 5 slices provolone
   cheese

Brown sausages in a non-stick skillet over medium heat; place in a slow cooker. Add pepper and onion; top with pasta sauce. Cover and cook on low setting for 4 to 6 hours. Place sausages in buns; top with sauce mixture and cheese.

Top bowls of soup with crunchy cheese toasts. Brush thin slices of French bread lightly with olive oil. Place on a broiler pan and broil for 2 to 3 minutes, until golden. Turn over and sprinkle with freshly grated Parmesan cheese and Italian seasoning. Broil another 2 to 3 minutes, until cheese melts. Yum!

Slow-Cooked Minestrone

Makes 8 servings

4 c. vegetable broth
28-oz. can diced tomatoes
3 8-oz. cans tomato sauce
3 c. water
2 c. carrots, peeled and sliced
2 c. celery, sliced
3 cloves garlic, minced

1 T. dried, minced onions
1 T. dried basil
1/2 t. dried oregano
1 t. sea salt
1-1/2 c. multi-grain rotini pasta,
   uncooked

In a 4-quart slow cooker, mix together all ingredients except pasta.
Cover and cook on low setting for 7 to 8 hours. About 30 minutes
before serving, stir in uncooked pasta; turn slow cooker to high setting.
Cover and cook an additional 30 minutes, or until pasta is tender.

It's a lovely thing...everyone sitting down
together, sharing food.

–Alice May Brock

Carly's Green Bean Casserole

Makes 6 to 8 servings

1 lb. fresh green beans, trimmed
   and cut into bite-size pieces
10-3/4 oz. can cream of celery
   soup

1/2 c. plus 2 T. milk
1 c. slivered almonds, divided

Place beans in a buttered 1-1/2 quart casserole dish. Add soup, milk
and 1/2 cup almonds; stir thoroughly. Top with remaining almonds.
Bake, uncovered, at 375 degrees for 30 minutes, or until hot
and bubbly.

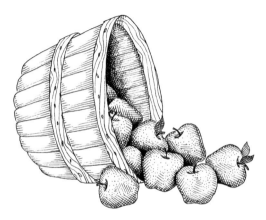

To give your warm-from-the-oven bread a sweet, shiny glaze, brush with honey...it also absorbs moisture and bread will stay fresh longer.

Applesauce Spice Muffins

Makes 12 servings

2 c. biscuit baking mix
1/2 c. milk
2 T. sugar
1/4 c. applesauce

2 T. brown sugar, packed
1/2 t. cinnamon
1/2 t. nutmeg

Combine all ingredients in a medium bowl; stir together for one minute with a wooden spoon. Fill greased muffin cups 2/3 full. Bake at 350 degrees for 15 minutes.

Making your favorite casserole? Make an extra to freeze...
enjoy the next time you need a quick dinner!

Salisbury Steak

Makes 6 servings

1-1/2 lbs. ground beef
1/4 c. round buttery crackers,
    crushed
1 egg, beaten
1 onion, chopped
10-3/4 oz. can cream of
    mushroom soup

1 T. mustard
1 T. horseradish sauce
1 t. Worcestershire sauce
1/2 c. water
2 T. dried parsley

Combine ground beef, crackers, egg and onion; set aside. Mix soup, mustard and sauces together in a medium bowl; add 1/4 cup to meat mixture. Form meat into 6 patties; brown on both sides in a skillet and drain. Stir water and parsley into remaining soup mixture; pour over patties. Simmer for 20 minutes.

Be sure to pick up a pint or two of ice cream in cinnamon, peppermint and other delicious seasonal flavors when they're available. What a special touch for holiday desserts!

Grandma's Gingerbread Cake

Serves 12 to 15

3 c. all-purpose flour
1 t. baking soda
1 t. ground ginger
1 t. ground cloves
1 t. cinnamon

1 c. brown sugar, packed
1/2 c. margarine, melted
1 c. molasses
2 eggs
1 c. boiling water

In a large bowl, sift together flour, baking soda and spices; set aside. In another bowl, stir brown sugar into melted margarine. Add molasses and unbeaten eggs; beat well. Add flour mixture and boiling water to brown sugar mixture alternately in small amounts, beating thoroughly after each addition. Pour batter into a greased 13"x9" baking pan. Bake at 350 degrees for 25 minutes, or until a toothpick tests done. Cool; cut into squares.

Mom's best advice for success in the kitchen...read through the recipe first! Make sure you have all the ingredients, equipment and time needed to make the recipe. You'll be glad you did!

Tangy Tuna Melt

Makes 2 servings

5-oz. can tuna in water, drained
    and flaked
1 T. mayonnaise
1 t. mustard

cracked pepper to taste
4 slices whole-grain bread,
    toasted
2 slices American cheese

In a bowl, combine tuna, mayonnaise and mustard; season with pepper. For each sandwich, spread half of tuna mixture on one slice of toast; add a cheese slice and top with another slice of toast. Place on a broiler pan; broil just until cheese melts.

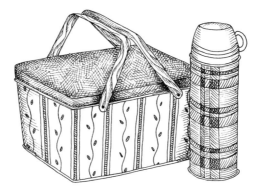

Packing a salad for a picnic or in lunch boxes? Freeze a few juice boxes and they'll keep the whole lunch cool!

Redskin Potato Salad

Makes 6 to 8 servings

8 to 10 redskin potatoes, cooked
and cubed
2 to 3 green onions, chopped

1 to 2 c. ranch salad dressing
salt and pepper to taste

Combine potatoes and onions in a large bowl. Stir in ranch dressing;
season with salt and pepper. Serve chilled.

For simple table decorations, place round pebbles in the bottom of Mason jars and fill with water. Then tuck in bunches of sweet daisies or sunflowers and tie a bow around jar necks with jute.

Chuckwagon Casserole

Makes 6 servings

1 lb. lean ground beef
1/2 c. onion, chopped
1/2 c. green pepper, chopped
15-1/2 oz. can mild chili beans
   in sauce

3/4 c. barbecue sauce
1/2 t. salt
8-1/2 oz. pkg. cornbread mix
11-oz. can sweet corn & diced
   peppers, drained

In a skillet over medium heat, cook beef, onion and pepper until no longer pink; drain. Stir in chili beans, barbecue sauce and salt; bring to a boil. Spoon into a lightly greased 13"x9" baking pan and set aside. Prepare cornbread mix according to package directions; stir corn into batter and spoon over beef mixture. Bake, uncovered, at 400 degrees for 30 minutes, or until golden.

Pick up a stack of retro-style plastic burger baskets. Lined with crisp paper napkins, they're still such fun for serving hot dogs, burgers and fries.

Best-Ever Chili Dogs

Serves 8 to 10

8 hot dogs
2 15-oz. cans chili without
    beans
10-3/4 oz. can Cheddar cheese
    soup

4-oz. can chopped green chiles
8 hot dog buns, split
3/4 c. onion, chopped
1 to 2 c. corn chips, crushed
1 c. shredded Cheddar cheese

Place hot dogs in a 4-quart slow cooker; set aside. In a bowl, combine chili, soup and chiles; spoon over hot dogs. Cover and cook on low setting for 4 to 5 hours. Serve hot dogs in buns, topped with chili mixture, onion, corn chips and cheese.

For the tenderest muffins and quick breads, stir batter
just until moistened...a few lumps won't matter!

Lemon-Rosemary Zucchini Bread

Makes 2 loaves
or 2 dozen muffins

3 c. all-purpose flour
1/2 t. baking powder
2 t. baking soda
2 T. fresh rosemary, minced
2 eggs
1-1/4 c. sugar

1/2 c. butter, melted and slightly
  cooled
1/4 c. olive oil
1 T. lemon zest
3 c. zucchini, grated

In a bowl, whisk together flour, baking powder, baking soda and rosemary; set aside. In a separate large bowl, beat eggs until frothy; whisk in sugar, melted butter and olive oil. Stir in lemon zest and zucchini. Add flour mixture to egg mixture; stir until blended. Divide batter into two 9"x4" loaf pans sprayed with non-stick vegetable spray. Bake at 350 degrees for 45 to 50 minutes. May also spoon batter into 24 paper-lined muffin cups, filling 2/3 full; bake at 350 degrees for 20 minutes.

Thank God for dirty dishes,
They have a tale to tell.
While others may go hungry,
We're eating very well.

Author Unknown

Easy Italian Wedding Soup

Serves 4

2 14-1/2 oz. cans chicken broth
1 c. water
1 c. medium shell pasta,
    uncooked

16 frozen meatballs, cooked
2 c. fresh spinach, finely
    shredded
1 c. pizza sauce

Bring broth and one cup water to a boil in a large saucepan over medium-high heat; add pasta and meatballs. Return to a boil; cook for 7 to 9 minutes, until pasta is tender. Do not drain. Reduce heat; stir in spinach and pizza sauce. Cook for one to 2 minutes, until heated through.

A crockery bowl filled to the brim with
ripe apples and pears makes a simple centerpiece...it's a
great way to encourage healthy snacking too!

Lillie's Fruit Salad

Serves 4 to 6

8-oz. can crushed pineapple in juice
2 ripe bananas, sliced

1 to 2 Red Delicious apples, cored and diced
1/2 c. orange juice

In a large bowl, combine all fruit. Add enough orange juice to cover fruit; mix gently. Cover and keep refrigerated.

INDEX

INDEX

Our Story

Back in 1984, we were next-door neighbors raising our families in the little town of Delaware, Ohio. Two moms with small children, we were looking for a way to do what we loved and stay home with the kids too. We had always shared a love of home cooking and making memories with family & friends and so, after many a conversation over the backyard fence, **Gooseberry Patch** was born.

We put together our first catalog at our kitchen tables, enlisting the help of our loved ones wherever we could. From that very first mailing, we found an immediate connection with many of our customers and it wasn't long before we began receiving letters, photos and recipes from these new friends. In 1992, we put together our very first cookbook, compiled from hundreds of these recipes and, the rest, as they say, is history.

Hard to believe it's been almost 40 years since those kitchen-table days! From that original little **Gooseberry Patch** family, we've grown to include an amazing group of creative folks who love cooking, decorating and creating as much as we do. Today, we're best known for our homestyle, family-friendly cookbooks, now recognized as national bestsellers.

One thing's for sure, we couldn't have done it without our friends all across the country. Each year, we're honored to turn thousands of your recipes into our collectible cookbooks. Our hope is that each book captures the stories and heart of all of you who have shared with us. Whether you've been with us since the beginning or are just discovering us, welcome to the **Gooseberry Patch** family!

Jo Ann & Vickie

Visit our website anytime
www.gooseberrypatch.com

Email

1·800·854·6673